KENTUCKY BOUND: poems, stories & songs

No matter where I wander
No matter how far I roam
The most beautiful place on the planet
Is always singing my song
calling me home
The place and the people shaped me
Helped make me who I am
Until the day I die I'll be thankful
I'm forever Kentucky bound

OTHER BOOKS BY RON WHITEHEAD

A Taoist Nun Teaches Me in Fourteen Poems
Beaver Dam Rocking Chair Marathon
blistered asphalt on dixie highway: Kentucky Basketball Is Poetry in Motion
Blood Filled Vessels Racing to the Heart
Disobey
EVE & The OPHIDIANS
Ghost Lover, Trance Mission
I'd Never Shoot a Man While He's Washing Dishes: Arcturian Love Songs
I Refuse I Will Not Bow Down I Will Never Give Up
I Will Not Bow Down
Kokopelli
Mama: a poet's heart in a Kentucky girl, photo edition
MAMA: a poet's heart in a Kentucky Girl
Quest for Self in the Ocean of Consciousness: Ibsen, Hamsun, Munch, Joyce: The Origins of Modernism and Expressionism
Searching for Jack Kerouac
The Declaration of Independence This Time: Selected Poems
The Path of the Ancient Skald
The Storm Generation: Poems by Outlaw Poet Ron Whitehead
The Storm Generation Manifesto & On Parting
The Third Testament: Three Gospels of Peace
The Wanderer
We See the Sound of Setting Sun
Western Kentucky: Lost & Forgotten, Found & Remembered

AUDIO RECORDINGS BY RON WHITEHEAD

DRAGONS
Exterminate Noise
Frogg Corpse & Mr. Stranger Present The End of the World
From Iceland to Kentucky & Beyond
I Refuse
I Will Not Bow Down
Kentucky Blues
Kentucky Roots
Kentucky: poems, stories, songs
Pack My Soul in Dry Ice
Prayer
Ron Whitehead and Southside's Southside Lounge
Ron Whitehead and Southside's We Are the Storm double-CD
Searching for Jack Kerouac
Songs & Poems from the Kentucky Bound Concert
Swan Boats @ Four
Tapping My Own Phone
The Bonemen
The Shape of Water
The Storm Generation Manifesto & On Parting, the Wilderness Poems
The Storm Generation Manifesto & Other Rock n Roll Poems
The Viking Hillbilly Apocalypse Revue
Trance Mission
Walking Home

KENTUCKY BOUND:
poems, stories & songs

Ron Whitehead

TRANCEMISSION PRESS
Historic Clarksville, Indiana

Some of these poems and stories have appeared in other publications, too numerous to mention, around the world. Thank you to each and every publisher.

Editors: Ron Whitehead and Jinn Bug
Layout, graphic design and production by Jinn Bug
Original cover art, "Cradle to the Grave: Kentucky Bound",
traditional folk, 24x36', mixed media on canvas,
by Jeremy Scrimager, used with permission of the artist

Copyright © 2018 by **Ron Whitehead**

All rights reserved. No part of this publication may be reproduced, distributed or transmitted in any form or by any means, without prior written permission.

Trancemission Press
301 S Clark Blvd
Clarksville IN 47129
www.trancemission.xyz

Kentucky Bound: poems, stories & songs, Ron Whitehead
– 1st ed.
ISBN-13: 978-1726837613

Contents

Mama 1
Sex Education 2
Quilting in Deep Snow 4
A Master of Checkers 7
Pappy 9
Under the Wild Plum Tree Breathing Hard I Hide ... 13
The Pissing Contest 14
The Night Watch 15
The Sound of Snowflakes on Christmas Eve 19
In Snow In Rain In Cold In Gloom In Kentucky We Deliver 22
The Little Old Lady with the Giant Mole 23
Aunt Rena Dipped Snuff 25
The Hanged Man 28
Milking Her through the Fence 31
The Blood in My Brain Began to Sing 35
Old Man Cherry 38
A Bullfrog in a Jar Full of Vaseline 40
Mammie Got Hooked on Valium and Conrad Played the Fiddle 43
Dog, Sky 46
The Wild Dogs of Kentucky 47
Music Saved My Life and Jesus Saved My Soul/The Impossible Dream 50

Granddaddy's Death Taught Me How to Live 54
10 Foot Shots on an 8 Foot Goal 57
The Centertown Baptist Church Haunted Hill Graveyard 58
Little League Baseball and PLAYBOY Magazine 61
Coffee, Tobacco, DDT, and Me 63
"Jambalaya" 66
Moxley and Eirene 68
Riding Bareback 70
My Life in Golf 71
Moxley and Eirene Moonshine King Burgoo Queen 74
Wrestling Hercules 79
Grade School Classroom Layup 81
Stevie Fell Out 82
Rags 84
Getting Cut 87
What Came Out of the Barn 89
Popcorn Adolf Rupp Larry Conley Tom Jones and My Brother Brad 92
Thanksgiving in Kentucky 94
Miss Myrtle Calvert 98
Breaking and Entering Basketball 99
"Boys It's Time to Hoe!" 100
Mama and Daddy Taught Me 102
Daddy, Curve Balls, and Overcoming Pain 103
Tobacco Sticks Coal Pucks Ice Hockey on Our Frozen Ponds 107
Square Bales Ain't Square and Neither Am I 108
Mourning My Father 110

Spadge Tooley Had Webbed Fingers	111
Aunt Sis Was a Saint	114
Otley Casteel	116
Learning to Swim in the Deepest River in the World	120
Kentucky Blues	123
The Loneliest Picture I've Ever Seen	126
Mama, a Poet's Heart in a Kentucky Girl	128
Arriving	130
Kentucky Haiku	132
About the Author	139

Mama

Mama killed chickens. She popped their heads off. Put her foot on the little hen's head, grabbed its legs and jerked hard. The head just laid there on the grass while the little chicken body went flopping all over the yard. Us kids ran like crazy dodging chicken blood. I liked it better when Mama took the .22 rifle to the barn and would shoot a little hen off the high rafter up near the top of the barn where the chickens all roosted. Mama was a good shot.

One Christmas Eve there was a terrible storm. Daddy was off at the mines. Mama said "come on" and all us kids piled into the back of the old pickup truck. Mama had the shotgun. We drove slow through the storm with Mama looking all round then she pulled over and said "come on." We followed. We walked a ways until we came up on a tree, a cedar tree, and Mama said "get behind me." We did and she took aim and shot the tree in the trunk with both barrels. Blew it clean in two. Mama said "y'all get the Christmas tree and come on."

Us kids let out a yell! We were so happy cause Christmas had finally come.

Sex Education

Daddy came home from the mines every day after
4 o'clock and no matter where on the farm we were

we'd tuned our ears to hear his truck comin' from
at least two miles away and the first to hear it always

yelled "Here comes Daddy!" and no matter what
we were doin' we'd run to hide and I knew the 1st

thing Daddy would yell when he set foot on the
ground out of the truck was "Ronnie come here!"

and the questions would start bout what work we'd
done today and if one thing hadn't been done or

even done but not done right then I'd get my daily
dose of beatin' and it took me years and years to

heal those bleedin' wounds but that's not all I remember
cause there were a handful of mornin's before Daddy

went to the mines when he'd come up to our attic
room and I still hear the steps creakin' with his big

footsteps walkin' up them and he'd put his hand on
our heads on those rare mornin's and Daddy said

"Boys it's time to get up" and in that brief touch and
those gentle words I felt and heard his love and it was

those memories that more than anything helped the
healin' once it finally happened but I also remember

that spring mornin' when Brad and I were standin'
behind the barn with Daddy and that was the day we

received our sex education when we all three looked
across the pond where the bull had mounted the cow

and Daddy said "See that?" and Brad and I looked
at each other and together said "Yeah!" and Daddy

said "Alright then" and in one fluid movement Brad
and I looked from the bull and the cow goin' at it and

then up to Daddy then to each other then back to the
bull and the cow goin' at it and the sky is turquoise blue

and it fills my soul and a crow caws up there somewhere
and I hear a whippoorwill down in the meadow and the

beagles are barkin' and it's such a beautiful spring day
and I'm glad to be alive and yes that's my formal sex

education and I reckon that's all I needed but it wasn't
long after that I started goin' to the library and hidin' in

a corner readin' whatever book on sex I could get my
hands on cause I just had to know

Quilting in Deep Snow

I sat near the open fireplace
playing army with toy soldiers

As the red orange and yellow
wood fire snapped crackled and popped

I glanced to the snowflaked panes
Through the frosted window

early January ice and snow
was whirling into a blizzard

The fresh coffee and cinnamon rolls
smelled delicious but suddenly

I was more interested in the story
Mammie Igleheart was sharing

with Mamaw and Aunt Rena
and Miss Haddie and Mama

as they quilted
"My little Reno was 4 years old

Daddy had a wood shed at the end
of the yard where he kept dry wood

and the sharpest ax you have ever seen.
One day Reno got the ax out

and split his foot open.
Scared us all to death.

I put medicine on his foot
and for days he was awful sick.

Blood poison developed in his body
and he died.

He was so quiet and pretty.
Little blue pants and white shirt.

And a tie like Buster Brown
tied in a bow.

When he was so sick and dying
he said "Do you see those ladies

dancing up there?" and he was looking
straight up toward the ceiling.

His death about killed me.
And I was pregnant

with little Ruthie.
She was born the next month."

Then Mammie Igleheart stopped talking
and started sobbing crying hard

Mama held her
The snow and ice fell harder

The fire crackled and popped louder

A Master of Checkers

On a snow drifting wind yelping wild nature Kentucky
winter's night Daddy said come on boys and we followed

Me worrying about Mama hoping she would be safe
Left by herself there on the farm while we went to hang

out with the men at Gene Lee's Centertown Garage old
iron coal stove Pay Day candy bars small bottle Coca

Colas Old Man Cherry and Spadge Tooley sitting on broke
down rigged up chairs with an upside down five gallon

bucket between them serving as table for checkers
The winner keeps playing as the other men take turns in

the loser's seat the old timers exchanging local gossip
and telling stories stories stories and I'm a shy boy at

least around these men but I'm forever listening to every
syllable watching each subtle nuance then the inevitable

questions are directed at me and Daddy says speak up
Ronnie and I respond with one line answers yet over a

decade of growing up winter nights at Gene Lee's
Centertown Garage sitting near the old iron coal stove

I too became a storyteller and
a master of checkers

Pappy

When we turned off Main Street onto the winding lane that led to the tent Daddy turned the Chevy's lights off and said

"Don't say anything." I called myself Bone Boy and my brother Muscle Boy. My brother was a miniature of my Dad who, instead of Edwin, could have been called Hercules. My Dad was tall and solid as rock. He believed in physical discipline so when he told us boys to do something we did it.

The light was bright inside the tent. The door was open wide to let in air. The night was hot and I imagined that it was hotter inside. Most of the people inside had walked. There were only a few cars outside the tent.

We pulled up close. It was a moonless, starless night so we weren't seen as we parked. My Father's Father, Jasper, Pappy, was standing at the microphone on the podium. Daddy turned the car off. Jasper was preaching:

> "But he that believeth not shall be damned. And these signs shall follow them that believe; In my name shall they cast out devils; They shall speak with new tongues; They shall take up serpents; and if they drink any deadly thing, it shall not hurt them; They shall lay hands on the sick, and they shall recover."

Jasper was a coal miner, a farmer, and a Holy Roller preacher. He was built like a hinged stone. The inner lights reflecting off the green canvassed tent cast a green glow about him, or was he casting the glow? If not casting he was certainly digging, digging for something hidden, pausing, deep in this green cavern, to proclaim:

> "Was I wrong? does this path
> Not lead to the light?
> But the light blinds my eyes
> If I seek it in the mountains.
> No, I must go down into the dark.
> Eternal peace lies there.
> Heavy hammer, break me the way
> To the heart-chamber of what lies hidden there."

Jasper's voice was getting louder. He was beginning to shout. Something I didn't understand was happening. I got a bitter taste in my mouth as I watched my Grandfather lose control.

Jasper was shouting louder and louder and becoming animated like I had never seen him. I imagined the bitter iron taste to be the water Pappy told me he drank that seeped from the walls deep in the mines.

A wailing moaning sound came from a little woman near the back of the crowded tent. Before her moan ended another began and then another and another echoing through the tent escaping out to me and Muscle and Daddy, through us, out into the dark night.

In the midst of the wailing a man shouted and then another and another until all the men were shouting. All the women wailing. And now a child's voice sang out in the chaos. Now more children. A chorus. Everyone stands, some on chairs. Now a guitar joins in. Now two. Now three. Three guitars. People begin to move, to shift and sway. Now I hear a piano. Now a tambourine. The wailing shouting singing playing grows louder and louder stirring the night. The swaying turns to swooping. Dogs bark, then howl. Lights in Centertown flash on.

Windows and doors open and heads peek out. Visions of The Second Coming dance in my head. I stare fixedly into the tent nearly hypnotized. An old man's swooping has turned into hopping. Another swooper becomes a hopper, then another. Women and children start hopping too. I don't understand the shouting. What words are these? Strange, unfamiliar. I don't recognize any of them.

A young woman falls down and starts rolling in the dirt jabbering strange words. Others fall and roll. Everyone is swooping and hopping and rolling, shouting and wailing and singing unknown sounds and words woven with the reckless music.

A dark figure appears from the back of the tent carrying a large black box. The figure approaches Jasper who is hopping and shouting on the podium. Jasper reaches into the black box and pulls out a rattlesnake

Oh Pappy

and he kisses the snake on its mouth

Oh my Pappy

I scream inside myself. Swaying and swooping and hopping and rolling and shouting and wailing and singing. Louder and louder and wilder and wilder.

The dark figure weaves the black box to men and women who take snakes: rattlers, copperheads, water moccasins from the box and perform the Jasper-snake kiss.

I see a man who looks like he swallowed his tongue. He is the tongue swallower. He makes no sound. He is rigid, white as a ghost, foaming at the mouth.

Daddy starts the car and without turning on the lights drives away.

Under the Wild Plum Tree
Breathing Hard I Hide

Wandering barefoot down the old dirt road
Saddling our raggedy western Kentucky farm
Seven years old 1958 blue jeans no shirt
Brown as dark buttered toast
Cobalt dragonflies swoop
Emerald June Bugs whir
Loudly singing "I wish I was an apple
hanging from a tree" when out of nowhere
A blue racer snake appears and chases me
Fast as our Appaloosa horse I run
In one long bound I leap the creek and
Under the wild plum tree breathing hard I hide

The Pissing Contest

On a hot summer Kentucky
Wild country backwoods afternoon
Tommy, Bruce, Stan, Brad, Stevie, and I
All of us boys one year apart
Me being the oldest Tommy being the youngest
Lined up
In the middle of a field
6 feet from a low lying
Electric fence
For a pissing contest
Whoever hit the fence 1st won
And there we went
6 rainbows of piss
Flying zooming towards
The electric fence
Next thing I knew
I saw Tommy flying backwards
6 feet
He landed hard on his back
Still pissing
After I said "Tommy Won!"
We all zipped our pants up
And rushed over
To make sure Tommy was all right
It took him a while to get his breath back

The Night Watch

i lifted my wind up alarm clock
from under my army cot
i was excited to have my own room
the long kitchen closet
as i stared at the baseball cards and pennant flags
tacked to the wood slat wall
i heard mama gently singing a sweet gospel song
i looked up to see her ironing clothes
there were clothes on hangers hangers hangers
and a waist high pile yet to go
the clock said 10:47pm

the night watch

i heard a truck crunching gravel on our long driveway
then 4 loud knocks on our blue front door
when mama opened the door 3 men stepped in
one said we need ed
daddy had slipped green khaki work pants
over his boxer shorts no shirt on
the upset man excitedly explained that
someone had been shot and
others beat up on the picket line

we need your help ed he said
the clock said 3:14am

the night watch

screaming tires screeching metal shattering glass
yet another wreck in front of our old farmhouse
on foggy nights folks missed the stop sign
where gravel road and asphalt road collide
peering out the front window i saw the rear end
of a car smoke and fire and a bloody face
with arms trying to crawl out of the gully across the road
racing out the front door daddy yelled stay here
the clock said 2:38am

the night watch

the telephone rang out in the night
mama answered she said ed it's the sheriff
yes daddy was a farmer and a coal miner
but he was also ohio county deputy sheriff
when the sheriff had a problem that was too tough
he called daddy who strapped on his holster and
loaded pistol put on his badge and cowboy hat and
said somebody's been hurt i'll take care of it go back to bed
the clock said 1:23am

the night watch

my eyes popped open as roy orbison
cranked all the way up
and another voice that sounded familiar yelled
ed bet you can't catch us then
as the jacked up red chevy nova revved its engine
i saw daddy slip out from the side of our house
he was in his boxer shorts no shirt
he had the pump action 12 gauge shotgun
which he aimed towards the car and
as he let out the howl of 10 madmen
the muscle car set fire to the road
keening teenagers moaning then screaming as
daddy unloaded the shotgun *kaboom kaboom kaboom*
blasting rounds skimming the top of the car he stood
now in the middle of the road as the scared kids fled
up the road and over the hill
with their hearts in their hands
the clock said 12:58am

the night watch

ed ed hey ed your bull's out
come on i'll help you get him back in
a man yells in the middle of the night
from somewhere out front
the front door slams
i didn't get up i stayed in bed
the clock said 4lordy08am

the night watch

the cedar wind whistled the pine wind whined
through the holes in the attic walls
my dead uncle ray visited me again a friendly spirit
stopping by to say hello and wish me well
dead relatives appeared often at the foot of my bed
in the attic room my brother and i shared
we had twin beds a lamp an am radio and
my wind up alarm clock on a night stand
the only furniture in our open raftered
unfinished floor bedroom the only place to walk
was from stairs to beds a vast open space
frequented by ghosts and singing winds
and my brother and me
it had snowed hard through the night
the house still moaned
i knew it was time to rise and shine i smelled bacon
mama was serving daddy breakfast i heard them talking
downstairs in the kitchen daddy was telling a joke
mama was laughing and i knew there would be no school
oh boy so i closed my eyes and stayed in bed
the clock said 5am

the night watch

The Sound of Snowflakes on Christmas Eve

1962. School was out for Christmas break. I was 12.
A little before dark, snow started falling.

It snowed all night.

Brad and I slept in the unfinished attic. Through the night
I listened to winter's wind whistling through the cracks

in our attic walls. I listened to winter's wind weaving
songs accompanied by the cedar and pine trees

surrounding and protecting our home.
Before daybreak I heard Mama and Daddy downstairs.

Daddy loading the furnace with coal then going out the
back door headed to the barn to feed the animals. Mama

in the kitchen cooking breakfast. She was singing, quietly,
"Oh Christmas Tree." I smelled bacon and biscuits and

gravy and coffee. Yes I was already drinking coffee.
Started when I was 6.

I woke Brad up. Brad was a sound sleeper. I said, "Hey, Brad, wake up. Let's see how much snow we got. Hey, get up. We've got to go milk the cows, chop the ice on the pond, and bring the coal in. Come on, Mama's cooking breakfast. I'm going down."

Brad and I had breakfast with Mama and Daddy. As always Mama's cooking was delicious. We ate every crumb. Brad licked his plate.

Daddy left for work at the mines.
After Brad and I finished our morning chores I got my .410 shotgun and went hunting.

It had snowed over a foot during the night and giant flakes were still falling. The snow wasn't letting up. I walked and walked and walked. I was in awe of the beauty, all the beauty that surrounded me.
I lost track of time.

I found myself in a field surrounded by woods. All around me the wind whispered through the limbs

the branches of the barren trees. The wind whispered
through the fur of the evergreen trees. A lone crow

cawed in the distance, searching its way home.
It was then I realized that I was hearing a sound

louder than any other, a loud but gentle and soft
sound, the sound of falling snowflakes.

That sound, that moment, comes back to me often,
including now, transporting me to a time and a

place long gone, but a time and a place that will
live eternally in me in my heart's memory.

In Snow In Rain In Cold In Gloom In Kentucky We Deliver

With tape measure and hand saw and hammer and nails
my brother and I built the 2 by 8
oak wood slatted backboard
We added the rim and threaded the net
Nailed each side to tall cedar posts
between farmhouse and barn on the south side of the yard
Next to our garden and orchard we dug 2 deep holes
Soon as daddy got home from the mines he helped us hoist
our new basketball goal into the ground and tamp it down
I got up during the night to watch giant snowflakes fall
But at dawn the flakes lightened and the temperature rose
School was cancelled so after breakfast
We swept the court and as we took our first shots
snow turned to rain the court became mud but
My brother and i played and played all day we played
In snow in rain in cold in gloom in Kentucky we deliver

The Little Old Lady with the Giant Mole

Once upon a time
When I was a little boy
There was a little old lady with a giant mole
On her right cheek
The lady was as sweet as could be
Her mole was so large
I had to continually fight my eyes
To get them to turn away from the mole
And look into her eyes
Her name was Minnie Igleheart
She was kin
Through Mamaw and her Igleheart clan
Granddaddy Render mail ordered 3 houses
from Sears Roebuck and Company
When Granddaddy and Mamaw
And their gazillion kids
My aunts and uncles
Moved to Valley Station
Which for years I thought was all of Louisville
We moved into the big Sears and Roebuck home
Granddaddy and his Render army had moved out of
The little old lady with the giant mole
Lived behind us in one of Granddaddy's Sears homes
Every time I visited the little old lady gave me candy

She gave Mama a big cookbook
Many years later Mama gave the cookbook
To my sister Velvet who still has it
When I was 5 years old
We moved to the farm
And I started my new life
As a wild nature farm boy
The little old lady with the giant mole
Minnie Igleheart
Died not long after
Mama and her sister sang at the funeral
Mama and her sister sang at every funeral and wedding
And they took us kids with them
That's why to this day
I often get weddings and funerals mixed up
I've always remembered
The little old lady with the giant mole
And I'll forever cherish her kindness

Aunt Rena Dipped Snuff

Aunt Rena started dipping snuff
When she was a girl
And she dipped all her life
Until she died
In her 90s
And she never got sick
A day in her life
She lived through
The Spanish Influenza
She outlived her husband
And her little boy
She nursed family and friends
Seeing them through all the way to dying
When someone got sick
Or was ailing at the end of their lives
Aunt Rena took them in
I visited her
And spent the night with her
Many times when I was a boy
When I was in 6th grade
I stopped by after school
And played my cornet
For Aunt Rena
And Mammie and Daddy Charlie Igleheart

Aunt Rena took care of them
The last years of their lives
She was a smart and big hearted woman
I loved Aunt Rena

The fireball explodes in the west
The air is honeyed
Katydids sing
Old women sit on their porches
Pinching snuff smoking pipes spitting tobacco
Watching the sunset remembering
Their dead children wondering about death
I know
I see them
I hear them
I sat with Aunt Rena for hours rocking
Listening to the fire crackle smelling corn
Baking on the fire listening to her stories
Listening to the silence
A mournful 94 year old Aunt Rena moans

"My little Roy was seven years old
When he went to school. It was
His first day. Going in he got his head
Caught in the heavy front doors
And he got a concussion and bleeding
In his head and in three days he lay dead."

Aunt Rena never forgot
She talked and cried
94
Seven
Rena and sad little Roy

Times at night when I was a boy
I listened to the wind whispering
Through the pines whistling through
The holes in my attic walls whispering

"Rooooy Rooooy" and I saw Roy
Walking across my unfinished attic floor
A fair and friendly boy
Roy

The fire flickers in the west
Almost out
Somebody better get some more wood
Is there resurrection in the wake?

When I see Aunt Rena dipping snuff
All her life
Helping others
A sweet and generous woman
A bright and shining soul
I believe in resurrection

The Hanged Man

Billy Joe Kitchens turned the curve
On the old dirt Whitehead Road
Heading to my Great Uncle Pete's
When he glanced over to his right
And saw the hanged man
Dangling from the maple tree
In front of the porch of his little house
Billy Joe turned screaming
"Hanged Man! Call Ed! Hanged Man! Call Ed!"
All the way back to Centertown
We were all in our farmhouse kitchen having dinner
When Daddy received the call
He said "Come on boys!"
And my brother Brad and I
Looked at each other
Then excitedly put down our forks
And headed out the door with Daddy
Daddy was strapping on his holster
With his always loaded pistol
Brad and I loved going with Daddy
On these out of the blue adventures
Daddy was Ohio County's Deputy Sheriff
When we got to the bottom of the hill
Daddy pulled into Alta The Gypsy Queen's driveway

I called her Red Headed Alta The Gypsy Queen
She was a wild woman
Mother of several children
And longtime family friend
I never knew what Alta would do or say next
And I liked that
Daddy said "You boys stay here with Alta!"
Which pissed me off
It always pissed me off when Daddy
Made us keep some distance from the crime scene
I liked it better when Daddy forgot
And let us go all the way up to where the action was
Which was usually the case
Daddy went running up the hill
With his pistol out
Brad and I watched him go
Then I looked past Daddy and saw
The hanged man
And that set my imagination running wild
Cause I had seen that old gentleman many times
And waved or said hello
He was a quiet and polite man
He kept to himself
I wish I had asked more about him
When I remembered him yesterday
I called Mama
Mama turns 87 on May 23rd
I'm taking her to the John Prine concert
At the Beaver Dam Amphitheater tomorrow night

Mama didn't remember any details
About the man's life
And Daddy died 9 years ago
So I can't ask him
I've long wondered why that gentle man
Hanged himself
And what dying by hanging must be like

Postscript: After my sister Edie read
this story she asked some of Alta's family
and this is what she discovered:
"His name was Mr. Royal. His wife died
and he became depressed. Went and sold everything.
Paid for his funeral. Bought a new pair of overalls.
And hanged himself."

Milking Her through the Fence

Johnny's dad had one hand and one leg.
Well actually Old Man Powers
had two legs but one was wood.
He had a big purple mole
on the side of his nose.
He smelled like stinkweed
and after his stroke
he drooled and his limp was worse.
Everybody said he was mean.
But the night he burned up
when his house burned down
I saw his wood leg burning,
a bright purple flame,
on what had been the living room floor
and I began to wonder.

The Powers' farm was next to Uncle Pete's
and I knew that Uncle Pete
had acquired 150 of his acres
from Old Man Powers.
Johnny was just born
and there was no food,
with the drought
and the coal mine being closed,
so no wage paying work,
and his Mom's milk had dried up.
Johnny's mom was a tiny woman.
Hard to believe she had eight kids.

Benjamin was the last one.
She died giving birth to him.
But Johnny was the oldest,
the firstborn, and he was starving.
He was crying hard,
his hunger was so strong.
So late one night
Old Man Powers slipped
out of the house
and crossed the fields to Uncle Pete's.

Old Man Powers said,
"Pete, my boy's starving.
He needs milk.
You got a milk cow
and I got land.
I'll trade you half my land
for that cow right now tonight."
Old Man Powers didn't tell Pete
he'd already been milking her
through the fence.

Uncle Pete just stared at him for a while.
Uncle Pete was a little slow.
Not stupid, just a little slow.
He was in his Scotch tape phase.
Someone had told him
that if he would tape his nose up
it wouldn't run so bad.
He had allergies
and his nose drained constantly.
He poked a hole in the tape over each nostril,

with an ice pick, to get air.
He wore the Scotch tape
for nearly ten years before giving up on it.

Uncle Pete finally spoke.
He told Old Man Powers, "Alright."
And they traded.
Went to town in a week
and drew up the deed.
One hundred fifty acres for a milk cow.
Saved Johnny's life.

Old Man Powers and his wife
had eight kids, all boys.
Had them all in eight years,
one right after the other.
Farmers who had anything back then
had lots of chickens and they'd wander
from one farm to the next looking for food
and just wandering like chickens do
and at night they'd find a safe place
to roost wherever they could.
The Powers had a trapdoor
in the living room floor.
At night they'd get a fishing pole out,
put a piece of soft corn on the hook
and drop it through the trapdoor.
The house sat three feet off the ground
like most farmhouses do.
Pretty soon they'd catch a chicken.
Oh, it'd put up a fight but not for long.
Once they got it up through the trapdoor

Old Man Powers snapped its neck to shut it up.
They'd pluck the feathers fast
and burn them in the kitchen stove
so there'd be no trace.

Johnny's dad had one hand and one leg.
Well actually Old Man Powers
had two legs but one was wood.
He had a big purple mole
on the side of his nose.
He smelled like stinkweed
and after his stroke
he drooled and his limp was worse.
Everybody said he was mean.
But the night he burned up
when his house burned down
I saw his wood leg burning,
a bright purple flame,
on what had been the living room floor
and I began to wonder.

The Blood in My Brain Began to Sing

In the summer of 1959
I was 8 years old
Barefoot and no shirt
Wearing cutoff jeans
I was sun brown
Climbing the highest tree
I could find
near the house
on our wild Kentucky farm
I loved to climb
It was Friday
and I was watching out
for my Render relatives
coming from Louisville
to visit for the weekend
We're a huge family
Mama's the oldest of 13
She was our mother
and she was 2nd mother
to all her sisters and brothers
We slept everywhere
On army cots
On couches
In chairs

On floors
8 to a bed
4 at the top
4 at the bottom
We slept
in tents
and in cars
Sometimes folks
slept in the hay
in the barn
Granddaddy and Mamaw
will be coming
over the hill
in the distance any second
They'll be followed
by at least 3 or 4 more cars
filled with Renders
and their families
and I'm gonna make sure
I'm the 1st
to yell real loud
"Here They Come!"
I loved to hear
my brother and sisters scream
while running all over the yard
"They're coming! They're coming"
And I had to be all the way up
in the top of the tree
so I'd be the first to see them

I climbed and I climbed
all the way up to where
the limbs were so thin
the branches
started to sway
back and forth
I had the best balance
I held on tight
I swayed
with the branches
in the breeze
high atop
the giant maple tree
and that's when
the blood in my brain began to sing
and my heart pounded with joy
and in that moment
I saw them
and I yelled
"Here they come!"

Old Man Cherry

I was playing checkers
With web fingered Spadge Tooley
At Gene Lee's Centertown Garage
It was winter
A bitter cold wind was whirling
Snow down Main Street
When Old Man Cherry stepped in
Proclaiming "It's colder than a witch's titty out there!"
Old Man Cherry was a jolly old soul
In the summer he and Spadge sat
Out in front of Glen Maddox's General Store
And in the winter they nestled
Near the potbellied stove
In the front room of Gene Lee's Garage
Old Man Cherry and Spadge were pranksters
Always telling stories and jokes
And pulling pranks on anybody and everybody
Well apparently Old Man Cherry
Had pissed Gene Lee off
Cause when Old Man Cherry sat down
In the old bent metal chair next to the potbellied stove
Gene Lee flipped a switch on the wall
And Old Man Cherry jumped out of that chair
Running over Spadge and me

Knocking us and our checker table over
Screaming "A woman's ass and a whiskey glass
Made a horse's ass out of me! Which one
Of you sons of bitches did that?!
You bastards shocked the hell out of me!"
Daddy and all the other men
Laughed their asses off
But I was bewildered
Not being in on the joke
Gene Lee finally confessed
That he had wired the chair
And made it go electric
When he flipped the wall switch
All the men had made sure
That was the only chair available
When Old Man Cherry came in
Retribution for all the pranks
Old Man Cherry pulled on Gene Lee and others

A Bullfrog in a Jar Full of Vaseline

There was a small swimming pool
under the church choir
Sometimes I wondered
what would happen
if the floor collapsed
while the choir was singing
our usual altar call
"Just As I Am"
all 17 verses
and they'd all
be swept into the pool
I wondered if they'd keep on singing

When I was a little boy
I got baptized in that swimming pool
under where the choir sang

It was magic
to come to church service
whenever it was time
for someone to be baptized
and the choir pews
were all gone
and the preacher in his white shirt

held the Bible in one hand
and read from it
while holding on to
a boy or a girl or a man or a woman
with his other hand
Then the preacher
carefully put the Bible down
on the floor
in front of the pool
and started talking like Jesus
Then he grabbed
the kid or the adult's face
and swept them down
into the water
and held them there
for a minute
then pulled them up
all spluttering spitting and spouting
and everyone in the church shouted
"Hallelujah!" and "Amen!"

And when it came my turn
to be baptized
to take the waters
to be dipped under
it was a big deal
I wondered what I'd see
Would I see Jesus?
I hoped to see Jesus

I prayed to stare
deep into the eyes of Jesus

And when I went under
it was impossible
to get my breath
The preacher
had his big hand
covering up my nose
and my face
and while I was down there
I saw many things
some of which were sacred and holy
but I've always wondered
why I saw
a bullfrog in a jar full of Vaseline

Mammie Got Hooked on Valium and Conrad Played the Fiddle

Mammie Igleheart got hooked on Valium
She talked more in those 2 years
Than she did the entire rest of her life
One morning she woke Daddy Charlie up
And said "Get up Charlie! We're going to North Carolina!
We'll ride the Greyhound! We're going to visit Conrad!"
Conrad was the son who lived
Reno died from an ax wound when he was a boy
Daddy Charlie said Mammie talked
With every person on that bus
Nonstop there and back
When Mammie was taking Valium
She stopped by to visit neighbors
And talked a blue streak
Nobody had seen anything like it
All her life Mammie had been quiet
But Conrad was a talker
Every time he came home from North Carolina
He brought his fiddle his mandolin and his guitar
He and Morgan Duncan were Mabrey cousins
Mammie's full name was
Bessie Baker Mabrey Igleheart
Her name was so long it wore her out
She decided to give her kids one name each

Louverine and Ruthie and Conrad and Reno
Conrad was a wild man
He was as good a fiddle player
As Vassar Clements and Art Stamper
Years later I read my poems in Nashville
Accompanied by Vassar Clements
And Willie Nelson's Band and David Amram
And a decade after that
I hung out one night in Shepherdsville
With Art Stamper and Ralph Stanley
Art had cancer
He sat in with Ralph for a couple of songs
After the show
On the way out the door
Art Stamper grabbed my hand
And looked deep into my eyes
His eyes watered up
He couldn't talk
That moment of holding Art Stamper's hands
And staring deep into his eyes
Was a mystical moment
Similar to my experience with The Dalai Lama
It was real strange
In the best of ways
I left the next morning
For an Ireland Performance Tour
Soon as I got back I read that Art had died
But I'm jumping ahead
When Conrad came home to visit

He said "Come on Ronnie! Let's Go!"
And we'd drive all over the country
Visiting this family member and that friend
With Conrad telling stories
And playing music and singing songs
He knew everybody and they loved him
I loved his wild spirit
It was a big deal when Conrad came home
One day Ruthie came down from Louisville
She was shocked by Mammie's behavior
She found the medicine bottle
She did some research
She had a Valium pill analyzed
She took Mammie to Louisville
And got her off the Valium
When Mammie came back home
She was her calm self again
Mammie Igleheart was one of the kindest
Gentlest people I've ever been blessed to know
It was a surprise to witness Mammie's
Drastic shifts in behavior
But I liked her both ways
Talkative and quiet
Mammie and her son Conrad Igleheart
Were 2 of my favorite people

Dog, Sky

A half mile down the road from our house
dog and I step from gravel to brown grass
then into waist high orange sagebrush we
move through tall leafless oak trees we
pause to listen to wind singing in evergreen
dog smells everything we balance unsteady
on the log bridge dog falls into the creek I
keep an eye out for any and all movements
near and far dog shakes himself dry we
come out of the woods and head up the
hill that overlooks our valley three fourths
of the way up right before the hill's tree line
begins I find a dry mossy spot in the sagebrush
dog following the scent of something had
already entered the forest on the hill but seeing
me stop he returns dog sniffs out his own dry
spot and we lie down ready for an afternoon
nap dog sleeps I stare up at the turquoise
sky and watch the solitary white cloud float
over momentarily blocking the sun the cloud
shapeshifts out of nowhere a crow appears
enters the cloud I wonder if it's lost

The Wild Dogs of Kentucky

Across the road from the front of our old wood slatted
grey weathered two storied farm house
was an overgrown sassafras and plum tree lined dirt road
that forever beckoned me into deep Kentucky backwoods
the wilderness road meandered a mile then split
with the right turn heading over
to Volney Barnes' 500-acre farm and country home
Daddy, Brad, and I passed Volney's cutoff
staying on the crooked dirt road
which quickly became a narrow dirt path
Daddy had the 12-gauge pump action shotgun
I had my .410 break action single shot .22 over and under
Brad had the .22 rifle
I was 9 Brad was 7
Daddy was the best hunter and fighter of anyone
anywhere and everybody knew it
including and especially Brad and me
Nobody and I mean nobody messed with Daddy
so when we rounded a bend in the narrow dirt path
and we looked to our left to see
a pack of wild dogs digging furiously
throwing dirt up past their rear ends
I paid close attention to Daddy watching him
bend down into a crouch

Brad and I standing on each side of Daddy
did the same then in unison the wild dogs
caught our scent and jumped out of that hole
they were digging I reckon looking for groundhogs
and they turned to face us hair straight up on their backs
teeth sticking out past their lips growling then stepping
one step at a time all of them together in unison
moving slowly surely towards us
then Daddy bared his teeth and started growling
louder louder than the wild dogs
then with one long stride then another
Daddy moved directly towards
the pack of wild dogs
Brad and me crouched down
moving stride for stride with Daddy
then Daddy started raising up
and then I heard a growl and a ferocious howl
like I'd never in my life heard
and it was Daddy doing it
and then he started running towards
the pack of wild dogs screaming
like I'd never heard him scream
and believe me I'd heard him scream
and that pack of wild dogs
had never heard or seen anything like Daddy
and all together they turned
with their tails between their legs
running to beat hell
and that's when Daddy

raised his 12-gauge pump action shotgun
and let go *boom* one blast *boom boom* another blast
boom boom boom another blast
peppering the pack of wild dog asses
as they raced faster than they'd ever raced before
headlong into the deep dark Kentucky backwoods

Music Saved My Life and Jesus Saved My Soul/The Impossible Dream

"Just as I am without one plea
But that thy blood was shed for me"

We were a gospel quartet Brad Steve Stan and me
Singin' our hearts out "The Impossible Dream"
Sunday mornin' service at the Centertown Baptist Church
After the preachin' and "Just As I Am"
Paige came up and smilin' said "Boys that was sure good."
And she added laughin' real loud
"and Ronnie you sure are animated."
And then Saundra Karyl chimed in with "Yes that was fine but Ronnie you were flat." And oh my oh my oh my
I went home swearin' I'd never sing again
And I didn't until I got in the car
turned on the radio and heard Elvis croonin'
bout some old Kentucky backroads
And I caught myself breakin' my promise
Singin'
So what if I was flat as a pancake
Music had saved my life more than once
And I knew then as I knew before and after
that I'd never abandon song
I'd never quit listenin' to the gift of God
Sweet music

And even if I couldn't in public
at least in private I'd keep on singin'
And well us boys Brad Steve Stan and me
well I believe all our lives were saved
more than once by music and I mean
every kind of music
We heard it all
Church music and funeral dirges
As Mama and her sister Jo Carolyn sang
Far back as I can remember
I see people climbin' on coffins
Includin' Pappy
Him tryin' to keep
Mammy from leavin'
him behind
Her lyin' there in the pine
Yes we heard gospel and blues and we heard
country mixed with traditional folk mountain
Appalachian goin' back to Ireland and Scotland and Wales
And we listened to Jimmie Rodgers
and Hank Williams and Woody Guthrie
and Raymond Render and Mose Rager
and The Montgomery Brothers
and Brother Matthew's Gospel Quartet
With my 3rd grade teacher
Mrs. Duncan bangin' on that piano like I'd
never heard in no Baptist Church and I got excited
Oh Lord can music make you feel this good?
Brought tears to my boy eyes and made

goosebumps run all up and down my back
and all over my body
Made my flat topped hair
stand up straight and tall
without no butch wax on it
And then came Elvis and my parents said
"Turn it off!" but they were glued too and
didn't couldn't move eyes starin' in disbelief
but excited like what in the world is this
And seemed like everybody felt that way
More excited than ashamed wantin' to be
part of that energy that we all know somehow
like music itself must be a gift from
some greater source and we all mourned his passin'
But I'm jumpin' ahead cause for our generation
Bob Dylan and The Beatles did it too
And in Stan's yellow Volkswagen
travelin' through one lane Ohio County bridges
at the speed of light with windows down
we kept the stereo loud as it would go
Cause we loved music Cause whenever
we had to turn from the pain of life the sufferin' of livin'
we always turned to music
As if music redirected
us towards God
As if music came from God
And every time we turned to music
life became bearable again
We thought about Resurrection again

We thought about Jesus again

"And that thou bid'st me come to thee
O Lamb of God, I come! I come!"

Granddaddy's Death Taught Me How to Live

Granddaddy
Raymond "Dick" "The Dixie Yodeler" Render died
when I was 8 years old
He was in an accident
He was a grader operator
building The Watterson Expressway
that loops all around Louisville
Granddaddy could do anything
but that day he got his grader on a steep incline
and it turned over on him
He lived for a week
then he died
Mama said he opened his eyes
and looked up into the distance
and said "Go to church for me."
Then he died
Granddaddy was the Father of 13 children
I loved him dearly
His death taught me how to live

When Granddaddy died
his sister Aunt Sis
had his open coffin in her living room
Folks came from miles around and hours away

to pay their respects by bringing food food food
and by sitting around the living room
and standing outside
and sharing the stories
of living with Granddaddy
and what a wild and remarkable man he was
and I listened to the stories
and I played with Uncles and Cousins
There was solemnity and laughter
There was deep sadness and awful terrible grief
There was heartache and crying
There was a river an ocean of tears
and there was joy and gratitude and singing
I stood next to Granddaddy
He there in his coffin
dead
And in my mind I spoke with him
I told him how much I loved him
and I thanked him for being my Granddaddy

And on the 3rd day we attended the funeral
For the funeral
Granddaddy's coffin was moved
from Aunt Sis's living room
to the Walton's Creek Baptist Church
The church was standing room only
and a thousand people waited outside
We lowered Granddaddy's body in his coffin
into the ground there

at the Walton's Creek Graveyard
and his body is still buried there

After all these years
I look back on that funeral
and realize that through laughter and tears
Granddaddy's death taught me how to live

10 Foot Shots on an 8 Foot Goal

Backyard full court
8 foot goal on one end
10 foot on the other
Grass worn down to hard dirt
10 foot rim leans to the left
and is too high in the front
8 foot rim sags in front
and leans to the right
It's time to order new nets
from the Sears catalog
and we keep pumping air
into the bald basketball
but all we care about is the game
5 on 5 shirts and skins
24 by 2 and 4 up to win
Winning team stays in
Keeps playing till the last glimmer
of sunlight is gone
Backyard full court
10 foot shots on an 8 foot goal

The Centertown Baptist Church Haunted Hill Graveyard

On Halloween night
In 1961
I was 10 years old
When my aunt Jo Carolyn
Said "Why don't we walk
Up the hill to the graveyard
And I'll tell you kids some true ghost stories"
Soon as she said those words
The hair stood up on the back of my neck
Cause I'd been there before
And I knew her stories were all true
So we slowly but surely climbed the haunted hill
To the Centertown Baptist Church Graveyard
And we huddled down
Squatting lower inch by inch finally sitting
On top of an old grave
I could barely make out the first name Jennings
But the last name was clearly Whitehead
My aunt Jo Carolyn leaned back
Up against the tombstone
And as the clouds drifted
Over the full moon
As the wind started whipping recklessly
Whispering then loudly pleading

Out of the lonely graves and through the skeleton tombs
My aunt Jo Carolyn told us a story
About a father who stood in his front yard
Departing for a long unexpected journey
On a full moon night
And the moment he hugged
His wife and three children
They stood open mouthed
Screaming at first without sound
As he vanished into thin air
Right before their bewildered eyes
And every year since that full moon night
If you go back to that house
Which still stands grief stricken below Centertown
On the Matanzas Road
If you stand in the front yard
On the right night
Which happened to be
The same night
We were sitting there on the old sunk down grave
In the Centertown Baptist Church Haunted Hill Graveyard
When there's a full moon
And our moon was full
Well you could hear that man that father
From some far off place yelling for his family
And you could hear his family
Somehow still in that same front yard screaming for him
And when my aunt Jo Carolyn
Got to that part in the story

She screamed so shrill so loud
Her scream caught my blood on fire
And made every hair on my head
Stand up straight and tall
Without no Butch Wax on it
And suddenly us kids were on our feet
Running and screaming
Faster and faster louder and louder
Jumping high over tombstones
Running fast and loud as our legs and lungs could go
Back to my aunt Jo Carolyn's home
In the deep dark valley below
The Centertown Baptist Church Haunted Hill Graveyard
Thankful to be alive having survived another Halloween

Little League Baseball and PLAYBOY Magazine

I told my brother Brad
And my cousins Steve and Stan
To wander around the store
Beaver Dam Drugs
While I stole
My first PLAYBOY magazine
It felt like I was stealing
All the gold in Fort Knox
That PLAYBOY magazine was a treasure
To us boys growing up on farms
In small town America
It wasn't long after
That we were playing
A Little League baseball game
The Centertown Demons
Against the Beaver Dam Beavers
When the Coach asked me
To run up the hill
And get some baseballs
Out of his new Ford Mustang
When I spotted the balls
In the back seat
I also saw a big thick black binder
On the floor behind the passenger seat

Out of curiosity I picked it up
And opened it
It was a year of PLAYBOY magazines
WOW!
Needless to say
It took me longer to get the baseballs
Coach asked me when I got back to the field
"Ronnie, where the hell have you been?
What the hell took you so long?
Throw those balls out
Come on boys
Let's play some baseball!"
All I could think was
I hope Coach asks me
To retrieve balls from his car
At our next Little League baseball game!

Coffee, Tobacco, DDT, and Me

When I was 5 years old
We moved to the farm
Where I lived until I left home
When I was 17
I started 1st grade when I was 5
I started drinking coffee when I was 5
Milk and lots of sugar
One cup was all it took
To satisfy my coffee thirst
Coffee with biscuits bacon eggs and strawberry jam
Then off to school
I never missed a day
I loved to play
To swing all the way up
Level with the bar
Then fly out soaring soaring
I learned how to fall
When I was 7 years old
I smoked my first and last tobacco
Relatives were down from Louisville
Spending the weekend
The entire house overflowed
With folks of all ages
Singing shouting talking
At the same time

Daddy and Granddaddy Dick
Were in the kitchen
Talking and smoking cigars
I asked Daddy
If I could smoke his cigar with him
He handed it to me
I took a big draw
And held it in
Next thing I knew
I felt deathly ill
I raced out the back door
And puked in the yard
I never had the desire to smoke tobacco again
But we raised tobacco
When I was a teenager
On hot summer mornings
I pumped and pumped up the sprayer
Then headed down and up and down
The tobacco rows
Spraying DDT
By the time I reached
The end of the first row
I was drenched
With morning dew and DDT
I believe the DDT
Changed my DNA
That's why I'm more alien
Than I already was
When germs see me coming

They run
Now I'm 67 years old
I drink my coffee black
I never smoke tobacco
And I glow
In the dark

"Jambalaya"

There was a man who helped
Us work on our Kentucky farm
His name was Billy Joe Kitchens
And that man was blameless and upright
One who feared God
And turned away from evil
There was born to him
One daughter and one son
Billy Joe had a speech impediment
He was married to my Uncle Pete's daughter
Yvonne who Billy Joe called Ebon
I was never quite sure if my brother Brad
Was trying to sound like Billy Joe
Cause when Brad was a boy
Instead of calling me Ronnie
He and Billy Joe called me Wawa
I called Billy Joe's son Little Kitchens
One Sunday Billy Joe brought his family
By our farm for an afternoon visit
At 5 years old Little Kitchens
Was a damn good guitarist and singer
He loved Hank Williams Senior
And knew most of his songs
Little Kitchens cussed better
Than most grownups I'd heard cuss

Wherever he went he took his guitar and
His rocking chair his chewing tobacco and
His Camel cigarettes
Daddy asked Little Kitchens
To sing us some songs
So Billy Joe set his son's
Rocking chair down in our dirt driveway
Right between the house and the barn
Little Kitchens was dressed in a cloth diaper
And brown cowboy boots it was a hot Sunday
He spit out his tobacco while tuning
His guitar and when his mother Yvonne
Came out the back door Little Kitchens
Said "Mama bring me a goddamn cigarette
and a glass of milk" Yvonne without missing
A beat turned around went back into the house and
Fetched the cigarette and glass of milk
After Little Kitchens took two long draws
Off his Camel and a long swig of unpasteurized milk
He lit right into one of the best versions
Of "Jambalaya" I've ever heard

Moxley and Eirene

Several miles southwest of Centertown, deep in the bottoms where the bobcats still roam, on a tight curve of Green River, the deepest river in the world, lived, in a wicked, crooked, dirt hut, Old Moxley and his wife Eirene. The island, called Toad's Island, rose above the Green. It had flooded only once, back in '37. Moxley's parents had come from Hungary and Eirene's from Greece in the 1800s.

When I was a boy I visited Moxley and Eirene from time to time with Daddy or Granddaddy Dick. We stopped by after running trotlines. Some city people might call them trout lines but we never caught no trout on them; we caught catfish, turtles, snakes, and eels.

Moxley and Eirene had an orchard and a garden but Moxley always said he lived on snake, snapping turtle, possum, and moonshine whiskey. I saw him eating and drinking all of them more than once and with his big red and purple nose I figured he was telling the truth. He kept his moonshine still right in front of the hut. They had a one-eyed black cat with no tail called Spit and a three-legged dog called Tick. Eirene was probably a witch but a decent one and by the time I knew her she may have forgotten most of what she once knew.

One evening late, after sunset, Granddaddy Dick and I were gliding down river back to the car. We had run the line and been to visit Moxley and Eirene and as always we had stayed longer than planned. Granddaddy Dick was drinking whiskey, Moxley had given him, out of the jug he kept in the bottom of the boat and he was chasing it with beer. He always talked more when he was drinking but there was something odd about Granddaddy Dick. He really never talked too much but it always seemed like he said a lot more than he actually did. His stories had a way of setting me to thinking. I found myself inside some of his stories and the next thing I knew Granddaddy Dick was adding stuff and his story became real and just took off down the road all on its own and sometimes I had to run and catch up or get left behind.

Anyway, we were paddling down the river to the car and Granddaddy Dick said, "As far back as I know Moxley and Eirene only been off that island once. Went in to Centertown one day. Moxley bought a little mirror. First time he'd ever seen one. He slipped it into his coat pocket but Eirene saw him and one day not long after their trip Moxley went fishing for snapping turtles. He didn't wear his coat. Soon as he left Eirene slipped the mirror out of his pocket. She was furious! The nerve of that man carrying the picture of an old woman in his pocket and him married. She threw the mirror as hard as she could at the fireplace and broke it into a thousand pieces."

Riding Bareback

On a wild nature Kentucky September afternoon
I bridled our big work horse
And road bareback
Out of the barn
Down the meadow
Across the fields
Heading to the woods

The horse had a mind of its his own
He started going faster and faster
I tried to slow him down
But despite my efforts
He stubbornly sped up
And when we reached the creek
He jumped high and long
And I went sailing
Flying flying off his back
And when I landed
My head hit a huge sandstone rock
And for a lightning quick instant
I saw stars then passed out

When I came to
It was nearly dark
The horse was gone
I walked back to the barn
Swearing I'd put that damn
Saddle on next time

My Life in Golf

My brother Brad and I paid $5
for a bag of golf clubs, tees, and balls
from our uncle who lived in Valley Station,
just off Dixie Highway, in Louisville's South End.
The golf bag included 3 PLAYBOY magazines,
tucked under the clubs, in the bottom of the bag.
It was a real deal.

Our uncle worked at Spot and Steal:
spot it in the daytime, steal it at night.
Our transaction took place
out of adult viewing, in the barn.

Two weeks later, when the coast was clear,
after we'd done our morning chores
and Daddy left for work at the coal mines,
Brad and I took the lawn mower
and the golf bag
and headed out of the barn,
through the wooden gate,
around the pound,
down the meadow,
through the barb wire gate,
and over the hill,
near the chicken coop,
to our largest cow pasture.

We mowed 3 greens
and dug a hole in each one.

We played 3-hole golf all day
until, suddenly, we heard Daddy's truck
coming over the hill,
home from work
at the coal mines.

Usually, the 1st one of us
to hear his truck yelled
"Here comes Daddy!"
and, afraid of getting a whipping,
for not doing all our chores,
or doing them
but not doing one right,
we'd run to hide.
But we were so busy playing golf
we forgot to listen out
for the sound
of Daddy's truck
coming in the distance.

I watched, nervously,
as Daddy got out of his truck
and came over to our 3-hole golf course,
in our biggest cow pasture.
Daddy said, "What in the hell
do you boys think you're doing?"
I said, "Playing golf."

Daddy demanded, "Where in the hell
did you get those golf clubs?"
I said, "We bought them
for $5 from Timmy."

I didn't tell him
we'd already hidden the PLAYBOY magazines.

Daddy asked, "Where did Timmy get them?"
I said, "I don't know."
Daddy said, "Take all this mess to the house
and give it back to Timmy
the next time you see him."
We won't be keeping stolen property here.
Ever!"

We did as we were told.
And that was the end
of my life in golf.

Moxley and Eirene
Moonshine King Burgoo Queen

Mama gave me a tin cup when I was a boy. Til I left home, when I was 17, I wore a thin rope, to hold my pants up. I've always been skinny. I kept my tin cup, and a knife with a bottle opener, on my rope. They both came in handy many times including, and especially, my last visit with Moxley and Eirene.

I was 16, a year away from leaving home, leaving home for good, leaving home forever. I'd come to visit Moxley and Eirene, traveling by boat, alone. I didn't know how many more times I'd have this opportunity. It was a crisp clear day in early September. The sad and glad of early fall filled me up. It felt good but it ached with loneliness too.

Some of you know that several miles southwest of Centertown, 27 miles from Owensboro, Owensboro, the self-proclaimed burgoo capitol of the world, deep, and I mean deep, in the bottoms where the bobcats still live, on an island on a tight curve of Green River, the deepest river in the world, with catfish that have swallowed children whole, the Green River, with nests of water moccasins in every cove, on a tight curve of Green River lived, in a wicked, crooked dirt hut old Moxley and his wife Eirene. The island, called Toad's Island, rose, peaking with a small hill, above the Green. It had flooded only once, back in '37.

Unlike most of the Irish and Scots in Ohio County, the fifth largest county, and one of the poorest, in Kentucky, home of Bill Monroe, the father of Bluegrass music, resting across the Green River from Muhlenberg County and Paradise, unlike most of the Irish and Scots Moxley's parents had come from Hungary and Eirene's from Greece back in the 1800's.

When I was a boy I visited Moxley and Eirene with Daddy or Granddaddy Dick. We stopped by after running trotlines. Some city people might call them trout lines but we never caught no trout on them: we caught catfish, snapping turtles, snakes and eels all of which occasionally found their way into Eirene's burgoo, the best, and most peculiar, unlike any other, burgoo in the world. Eirene was the burgoo queen. Although few will admit it, folks from miles away, including all the way from Owensboro, eventually found their way to Toad's Island, down on the Green River, and borrowed the recipes, which continue to be used on rare, private, and special occasions, for Eirene's burgoo and Moxley's moonshine whiskey. Moxley was the moonshine king.

Moxley and Eirene had an orchard and a garden but Moxley always said he lived on snake, snapping turtle, possum, and moonshine whiskey. By the time I was 16 I'd seen him eating and drinking all of them more than once and with his big red and purple nose I figured he was telling the truth. He kept his moonshine still right in front of their hut. They had a one-eyed black cat with no tail called Spit and a three-legged dog called Tick.

75

Eirene, I guessed, was probably a witch but a decent one and by the time I first met her, when I was a boy, she may have forgotten most of what she once knew. But she had remembered how to make burgoo, the most unusual and distinctively flavored burgoo I've ever tasted. Same was true of Moxley's moonshine. I can barely even approximate their magic recipes. I was a poor witness especially once Moxley began offering pouring his moonshine, God's Tears, into my tin cup. It was the smoothest hard liquor I've ever, in my entire life, tasted. My vision blurred as I watched Moxley on my left and Eirene on my right. Sometimes they became one, not too pretty, person. But, despite their strangeness, I always liked both of them so no matter how ugly they looked as one person it didn't matter, I didn't care, I just sat there watching and grinning and smelling while they brewed the burgoo and the moonshine.

Moxley poured in spring water which he collected running directly out of the side of their Toad's Island hill. He added pure cane sugar, cracked corn and malt. He always cut the first gallon with water cause it was so strong. It kicked harder than a mule or an udder sore milk cow. Sometimes he added burnt sugar and water to change the coloring. He did that for variety. While Moxley was cooking up his strange brew my attention wandered back and forth so I watched Eirene cook her burgoo too.

I watched her make burgoo several times, over the years, and it was always different depending on what she had available. This particular time, the last time I saw her make it, when I was 16, she killed a chicken, snuck up behind it and cut its head off before it knew what happened, then she plucked it and tossed it in, then instead of beef or pork, she added chunks of snapping turtle, possum, water moccasin, and eel. Even though fish isn't common to burgoo I'm pretty sure, despite the moonshine I'd drunk, that she threw in several pieces of catfish.

I'd brought her two rabbits I killed hunting with Daddy. I helped her skin them then she threw them in, bones and all, didn't even cut off their heads. Of course the pot, which was on an open fire in front of the hut, was filled with water from the river. She also mixed in some dirty dish water. For some reason I never discovered, before adding the water she first placed river rocks in the bottom of the pot. Once the water was ready she tossed in tomatoes, potatoes, onions, garlic, cabbage, peppers, carrots, corn, beans, peas, ketchup, salt, pepper, thyme, vinegar, sauces, homemade red wine, plenty of Moxley's moonshine, pinches of a variety of herbs, then she said words I didn't understand, maybe Greek, the language of her ancestors, and she said them like she was casting a spell.

It was spooky the way she chanted those words getting a glazed faraway look in her dark eyes. Good Lord I knew it was gonna be good. It always was. She cooked it for hours. I'm not sure how many hours cause I passed out.

When I woke up the sun had set. It was a beautiful starry night. The full moon was rising. A pack of wild dogs was barking way off in the distance, up river. Crickets, katydids, frogs, and lightning bugs brightened the night providing a brilliant sound and light show.

Eirene and Moxley handed me food and drink, burgoo and moonshine, best food in the world, bar none. We stayed up late, into the night, sharing stories, listening close to each other, to the bobcat's mournful wail, listening to the spirits walking the earth late, late at night when the veil between worlds disappears.

The next morning, just after daybreak, a buzzing fly woke me up. All three of us had fallen asleep on the ground, up close to the fire which had fallen to a dull ember, almost out. The sun was cracking the sky over the trees east of the Green. I rose, walked silently to my boat and glided away. It was my final visit, the last time I saw my dear ancient friends Moxley and Eirene, moonshine king burgoo queen.

Wrestling Hercules

Daddy was a mighty man a warrior the best
He never lost a fight he defeated all the rest
There's a Super 8 video somewhere
that Mama shot of my brother Brad and me
wrestling Hercules yes to me
Daddy was and will always be Hercules
One of Daddy's brothers was a sniper in Korea
a green beret then later became an agent for the CIA
One day when I complimented him on being
such a badass he looked me in the eyes
and said "No not me. It was your Dad who was
the badass. He taught us all there was to know
bout how to be tough. He never lost a fight
and he was in plenty. And during The Depression
our Dad, Jasper, gave Ed one shotgun shell
a day to bring home meat for the table.
So every day Ed went hunting
and every day he brought home what he shot."
So my friends when I say I was raised by
a 10th degree badass a 10th degree smartass
know that I'm not kidding. The 1st 17 years
of my life would make Marine Boot Camp
look like the Training School for Valet Parking
and that's nothing against The Marines
or valet parkers. Daddy taught me how to be

a warrior how to fight relentlessly. I saw him
get into several fights and yes he won them all.
And oh Daddy could tell jokes and stories
for days and nights without repeating himself.
He was a good neighbor. If anyone needed
help on a farm or at the mines Daddy was
the go to guy. And at home when Daddy was
in good spirits he liked to wrestle and box.
My brother Brad and I tried many times
to wrestle him to the ground but we never
could. He always won. In the Super 8 video
wrestling match Daddy ripped the rear end
out of his work pants. His boxer shorts are shining.
Daddy was a mighty man a warrior the best.
He never lost a fight. He defeated all the rest.
Wrestling Hercules

Grade School Classroom Layup

With 10 seconds to go
at the top of the circle
which was near midcourt
of small Kentucky
hardwood floor
Dundee school gym
I faked to the right
then cut to the left
going by my man
down the center of the lane
but as I went up for the open layup
I was pushed hard from behind
propelling me through the door
under the goal into the classroom
where we had changed into our uniforms
After tackling 3 wooden desks
I brushed off my bruises and hustled
to the foul line where I hit both free throws
We won the game 12 to 10
Grade school classroom layup

Stevie Fell Out

there were more than 20 of us piled crammed
squeezed front and back i was sitting on

mama's lap my brother brad was sitting
on my lap granddaddy dick was at the wheel

speeding up matanzas road to centertown
when the old ford swerved in the sharp

crow nose curve the back passenger door
popped open and stevie fell out when

granddaddy dick finally heard the backseat
voices yelling then screaming stevie fell out

stevie fell out the tires burned rubber skidding
as granddaddy dick slammed on the brakes

luckily it was autumn stevie brushed leaves
off his clothes and out of his hair as he

crawled out of the ditch then raced to the
car which he dove into head first thankful

to be alive and not left behind granddaddy
dick yelled somebody hold on to that boy

as tires squealed burning rubber again
the car filled with several generations

flew into the night

Rags

Rags went everywhere I went
If I rested in the early spring orange sagebrush
On the side of old Render hill
Half mile back of our farm up next to the woods
Rags rested by my side
We watched the clouds shape shift
When I talked Rags listened
When Rags talked I listened
True friends
Blood kin
Through the woods across the fields
Over the creeks down the dirt roads
Down the gravel roads
On the winding asphalt
Whether I was on foot on horse or on bicycle
Rags was always by my side
We were one
Rags wasn't a hunting dog
Rags and I were explorers
Rags and I were wanderers
I loved Rags
Rags loved me
Blood kin
One
One of the best friends I ever had

And I've been blessed
With many best brother and sister friends

One hot summer day
When I was a boy
Rags got run over by a coal truck
The coal trucks never stopped running
They all ran too fast
They were always overloaded
Spilling giant lumps of coal from home to Kingdom Come
Time and again I dodged flying lumps of coal
Big enough to kill anybody
The coal trucks tore up the roads
But nobody ever stopped them or slowed them down
Nobody ever did anything about them
Rags drug herself into a thicket
Across the road from our old farmhouse
The thicket was one of my homes away from home
I crawled in with her
For three days
I took her water and food
She drank a little water but she wouldn't eat
I tried everything to get her to eat
But she refused
She tried but couldn't
Rags stared deep into my eyes
I stared deep into her eyes
A deep knowing look

The saddest most pitiful eyes I'd ever seen
Ripped my heart apart
I stayed with Rags every minute I could
Except when I had to do my chores
And at night
When I had to sleep upstairs in my attic bed
I found an old worn out blanket in the utility room
And wrapped her in that trying to keep her warm
I got hay from the barn
And spread it under and around her
But nothing stopped her from shivering and shaking
Rags died in my arms
Tore me completely up
I held her and talked with her
I cried a river of heart broken tears
Lost a member of my family
Rags
Blood kin

Growing up on a Kentucky farm
In the heart of coal mining country
Was a gift
A gift beyond measure
A gift beyond words
Growing up I had many dogs
Everyone became a close friend
Every last one got run over by coal trucks

Getting Cut

Far back as I recall I've been
the leader the captain I've been
in charge of whatever's going on I've always
wanted and expected it to be that way
Any other way felt wrong but
has it always been that way well
of course it hasn't the reality is I've been
on the other side of winning so many times
I became a contemplative I journeyed inward
I've spent as much if not more time searching
on the inside as I've spent adventuring
on the outside For example my sophomore
year of high school well I was still
5 feet 4 inches tall when all Ohio County
high schools consolidated into one giant
1,200 student school and there I was 13
years old heading into puberty stepping into
many unknown worlds simultaneously and
while studying calculus and trigonometry my
algebra 2 teacher humiliated me in front of
the class by asking me to explain how I derived
my answer which I couldn't do up until then whenever
I saw a question I saw the answer so I turned
away from my teacher and about the same time
that happened I was the last man cut from

the basketball team I'd always been starting
guard and forever being the youngest in all
my classes having started 1st grade at 5 cause
I loved school and wanted to go and being the
youngest of all my friends them all well into
puberty I was wondering if I'd ever get there Yes
I was counting hairs every one of them and I was
praying "Dear God, please help me grow!" Then
puberty finally arrived and it was a nightmare
And when our schools consolidated I hated
school I went underground I became a pirate outlaw
I hid my thoughts and feelings No one understood me
And I kept telling myself I didn't want to be and
I would never be understood I would forever travel
alone And it took me years and years of hard
traveling to heal so many deep and bloody wounds
but I'm stubborn and underneath all my anger rage and
pain I wanted to be whole I wanted to be loved I
wanted to love so I kept on keeping on finding
ragged rugged broken paths to healing I
finally got sick and tired of
getting cut

What Came Out of the Barn

On a hot summer June night
When I was 7 years old
Granddaddy Render and his entire Clan
Drove down from Louisville
To spend the weekend with us
On the farm
Whenever Granddaddy Render was around
Music and stories and wildness
Filled everything up and running over
Including beds and couches and floors
So a half dozen of us boys
Decided to put up our tent
And sleep in the backyard
But the party was inside
So right before sunset
We got the tent ready
For whenever we were forced
To go to sleep
And went back into the house
Where we joined in on the fun
As everyone grew louder
Talking singing yelling at the same time
Well apparently us boys
Were the loudest of all cause
Suddenly Daddy yelled
"Okay boys that's it!
You're way too loud so

Get outta the house!
All of you run to the chicken house
And touch it and run back!"
Oh No!
The chicken house was way over in the field!
And it was a dark night nearly midnight
The moon wasn't even out!
But when Daddy said to do something
You better do it or you'd get a good beatin'
So I said "Come on!"
And all half dozen of us boys
Filed through the utility room
And out the back screen door
Into the backyard where I said
"We better run!"
And we all sprinted down the backyard
Past our tent
At the barn we flew over the fence
Ran across the meadow
Past the pond
Climbed over the barbed wire fence
Then ran as fast as we could
Across the field
To the chicken house
When every one of us touched it
We started giggling
Then I said "Let's go!"
And we reversed the journey
Gong as fast as our legs
Would carry us

Across the field
Over the barbed wire fence
Past the pond
Climbed the fence
And soon as we started
Racing across the yard
Back to the house
The most terrible howling scream
Any of us had ever heard
Came out from the barn
Every hair on my boy body
Stood straight up
We all turned together
And saw a gigantic white shrouded
Screaming Howling Clawing Grabbing Ghost
Running straight towards us
We all screamed "RUN!!!!"
And we crossed that backyard
Breaking every backyard
Racing record
We flew through the screen door
Back to the safety of the kitchen
Breathing hard we looked up
As Daddy walked in behind us
Laughing so hard he was crying
Daddy loved to scare
The hell outta us kids

Popcorn Adolf Rupp Larry Conley Tom Jones and My Brother Brad

Some folks become athletes
My brother Brad was born an athlete
2 years and 12 days after the Kentucky
Thanksgiving when I came along
on December 5th 1952
my brother Brad was born
There's a photo somewhere of 2 year old Brad
in Speedo style briefs lifting weights
In baseball Brad was catcher
In softball he was center fielder
In football he was running back
In basketball he played guard
Brad played center field like Willie Mays
Brad danced like Tom Jones
Brad was built like Hercules
And Brad loved popcorn
He was a popcorn fanatic
In 1967 Brad and I attended the Kentucky
Sweet Sixteen State High School Basketball
Tournament at Freedom Hall The same year
Big Jim McDaniels from Allen County-Scottsville played
The same year lightning fast Caneyville
from Grayson County made it to the Semi-Finals
We were on the floor near the court when Brad

excitedly said "I've got to have some popcorn!"
So we headed to the nearest concession stand
and bought Coca Colas and boxes of popcorn
then headed quickly back to our seats
Well lo and behold as we flew around a corner
we had to put on our brakes to keep from
running smack dab into Adolf Rupp and
Larry Conley Adolf handed Conley two 20 dollar bills
and Larry walked away Then as in the
blinking of an eye Brad ripped the top
off his box of popcorn then pulled out a pencil
which I didn't know he had then stepped
up and said "Mr. Rupp, my name's Brad.
May I have your autograph?" And well
Coach Rupp stared at Brad then grumbled
"I reckon so." And you know what my brother Brad
now has that Rupp signed popcorn box top framed
and displayed in his living room right over
the chair where he sits and eats popcorn while watching
UK Wildcat basketball on TV
Popcorn Adolf Rupp Larry Conley
Tom Jones and my brother Brad

Thanksgiving in Kentucky

Mama and Daddy are here in the kitchen with Mama's parents, Mamaw and Granddaddy, and some of their kids, my aunts and uncles: Adeline, Kendall, Linda, Becky, Donna, Danny Boy, Stevie, and Timmy plus my brother Brad and our sisters Paddy and Edie. Edie's just four months old. It's Thanksgiving. I turned seven today. Daddy's home from the mines. Thanksgiving Day. My Louisville relatives are visiting. I'm excited by all the family energy by the laughing the loud conversations the singing. We love music. There are many singers and musicians in our family. Mama and Granddaddy are singing *When They Cut down the Old Pine Tree*. Granddaddy is playing the ukulele. Daddy asks me to recite the Trees poem. In certain situations I'm shy but I finally find the courage.

Trees by Joyce Kilmer

I think that I shall never see
A poem lovely as a tree.

A tree whose hungry mouth is prest
Against the earth's sweet flowing breast;

A tree that looks at God all day,
And lifts her leafy arms to pray;

A tree that may in Summer wear
A nest of robins in her hair;

Upon whose bosom snow was lain;
Who intimately lives with rain.

Poems are made by fools like me.
But only God can make a tree.

I spend most of my time in nature and feel close kinship with trees so I memorized the Trees poem right after I first read it. Everyone is clapping and yelling. The kitchen is full of family. People fill the two doors, one leading to the utility room and the other to the living room. They're leaning in, looking over shoulders, to see and hear. I turn to Daddy. Do Hiawatha I say. I love that poem and I love to hear Daddy recite it.

"The Song of Hiawatha"
part XXII

Hiawatha's Departure

By the shore of Gitche Gumee,
By the shining Big-Sea-Water,
At the doorway of his wigwam,
In the pleasant Summer morning,
Hiawatha stood and waited,
All the air was full of freshness,
All the earth was bright and joyous,

*And before him, through the sunshine,
Westward toward the neighboring forest
Passed in golden swarms the Ahmo,
Passed the bees, the honeymakers,
Burning, singing in the sunshine.
Bright above him shone the heavens,
Level spread the lake before him;
From its bosom leaped the sturgeon,
Sparkling, flashing in the sunshine;*

*On its margin the great forest
Stood reflected in the water,
Every treetop had its shadow,
Motionless beneath the water,
From the brow of Hiawatha
Gone was every trace of sorrow,
As the fog from off the water,
As the mist from off the meadow,
With a smile of joy and triumph,
With a look of exultation,
As one who in a vision
Sees what is to be, but is not,
Stood and waited Hiawatha.*

Daddy knows the entire poem but he just recites the last section tonight cause it's a long poem and others are gonna sing and play. Everyone is spellbound by the music of the poem. I've seen TV and movie westerns but Hiawatha helps me look deeper into what I imagine the Indians are like. I wonder why they are called Indians. Who are they really like? This is a special moment here now listening to Daddy tell the poem, seeing everyone pay close attention listening to the story. I'm waking up to a new mystery, to many mysteries. I want to know about the lives of these strange people everyone called Indians. Why do I feel close to them?

I realize now that I'm a poet. My mind isn't sure what it means but my heart knows and that's enough for now. Daddy is a farmer and a coal miner. He's worked hard all his life for Peabody Coal Company and has never missed a day of work. He's the strongest hardest working man I've ever known. Daddy loves poetry. He knows many poems by heart. He encourages me to learn poems and I do. I already know quite a few. Daddy always asks me to do Word Power with him when the Reader's Digest arrives in the mail. Words, poems. The spirit in poetry brings Daddy and me close. My heart grows big. I hold back tears. I am thankful.

Miss Myrtle Calvert

She was Bone's all-time favorite teacher. She taught him 4th grade. She taught both his parents. She taught several generations of Centertownians. She rarely carried a book into the classroom. She told stories, held spelling bees, had blackboard math contests, took all students outside for recess three and sometimes four times every day, regardless of the weather. She also paddled hell out of anyone who didn't pay attention or disrupted class.

Junior Snodgrass rolled his own Bull Durham cigarettes. He lit them with wooden house matches that would strike anywhere, on anything. It was the last day of school, before Christmas break, when Miss Myrtle, seeing Junior's pants on fire, took off after him. Junior, seeing the look in Miss Myrtle's eyes, took off running. By the time she caught him the fire had burned a big hole in the seat of his pants. Big Foot Addington, Junior's friend, toughest young man alive who never went to a dentist who used a hunting knife, if he ever got a toothache, to cut out his teeth, reported Miss Myrtle's only response to the neighborhood boys. She said "I intended to ignite his rear end!" Nobody ever messed with Miss Myrtle Calvert.

Breaking and Entering Basketball

I broke into my first gym
when I was 9 years old
Through my boyhood my teen years
and into my 20s I played
breaking and entering basketball
Between dribbles I listened
for the sound of a Principal's
a Teacher's a Janitor's a Policeman's
footsteps in the hall
When I was 12 I wrote a letter
to the Governor of Kentucky
Louie B. Nunn
explaining the community benefits
of keeping school gyms open
at night and on weekends
anytime there weren't school
activities The Governor wrote back
saying he agreed but nothing changed
so I kept playing
breaking and entering basketball

"Boys, It's Time to Hoe!"

I'm 9 years old in early September 1959
home from a day in 4th grade with Miss Myrtle Calvert
Best teacher ever Centertown School
My brother Brad and I are playing pepper
in the front yard barehanded baseball
Throwing hard as we can 1st one to drop the ball loses
Our sisters Paddy and Edie
are playing with dolls when Mama yells
from back of the house
"Boys, it's time to hoe!"
Our one acre garden and two acre orchard
are on the southside of the backyard
tween our yellow farmhouse and red barn
Daddy will be home after 4 o'clock
so brad and I run to the barn
and get our sharpened hoes
Paddy and Edie beat us to the garden
They sit at the edge playing with dolls
Brad and I are chopping and digging
out crabgrass when I hear a loud
rumbling and roaring I look up to see
an overloaded log truck driving too fast
flying down the hill I'm staring as it gets close
to the front of our house when a chain snaps
Then in slow motion the most God awful

crash bam boom as logs fall from the truck
rolling over the road coming to rest
in our front yard I let out a deep sigh
glad us kids listened to Mama yell
"Boys, it's time to hoe!"

Mama and Daddy Taught Me

Mama and Daddy taught me
through actions more than words
to never look up to or down at anyone
That we're all in this together
Eyeball to eyeball Shoulder to shoulder
No matter what is going on around me
that's how I choose to live my life

Daddy, Curve Balls, and Overcoming Pain

Daddy taught my brother Brad and me
how to catch fast pitches bare handed
by playing pepper
by throwing as hard as we could
First with gloves on
Catching the ball
in the pit the pocket
so it burned and numbed the hand
Then taking the glove off
and catching the ball barehanded
Giving a little when the ball hit the hand
Daddy taught us how to catch
the short hop ground ball
How to get down and stay down on grounders
How to keep our eyes wide open
and never turn our heads
even if we got hit in the face
Sacrifice the body
No matter what
keep the ball in front of you
Daddy knew baseball inside and out
He was a master coach of the game
He taught me how to throw a curveball
In one Little League tournament game
I struck out 19 of the 21 Rockport batters

I was pitcher Brad was catcher
Daddy stood with friends
right behind home plate
Daddy yelled at Brad and me during games
He always wanted us to play our best
Daddy bragged about my pitching in that game
for the rest of his life
A week later
in a Centertown versus Hartford game
I threw one of my best curveballs
to Buddy Hazelrig
and he blasted it
over the center fielders head
for a home run
As he rounded third base
Buddy yelled "Hey Whitehead,
throw me that same curveball next time!"
Early on I learned how to win
and how to lose
I learned that good sportsmanship
is more important than winning or losing
At 8th grade graduation
I delivered a speech titled Good Sportsmanship
My sophomore year of high school
I threw my arm away
by throwing too many curveballs
For a long time
the doctor talked
about putting a pin in my elbow

I had to quit pitching
but I didn't stop playing
I moved to 2nd base and shortstop
I had to warm up longer
I had to throw until my elbow was numb
so I felt no pain during the game
I learned a long time ago
how to play how to work how to live with pain
My brother Brad was a natural athlete
He was catcher and infielder in Little League
He pitched a few games
and I caught
I learned important lessons from catching
I learned how to keep my eyes open
when the batter swung the bat
Later on that helped me in many ways
including driving fast
passing vehicles
on one lane bridges
down old country roads
I learned how to keep my eyes wide open
and look directly at the person or situation
no matter who the person or what the situation
I have always had the tendency
to think too much
It's a natural state of being for me
I've learned how to relax and feel
Get out of my mind and into my body
Allow my sixth sense my intuition

to guide me
Learning that helped me become
a better athlete
Daddy and curveballs
taught me so much about life
how to keep my eyes wide open
how to not allow pain
to keep me from
playing the game

Tobacco Sticks Coal Pucks Ice Hockey on Our Frozen Ponds

In January of 1964
the temperature was zero all month long
My brother Brad and I made the best
of all situations so early one morning school was out and
Daddy had left for the mines and we'd done our chores
Spreading hay for the cows in and behind the barn
Chopping 1 foot deep by 3 feet wide holes
in the foot deep ice
on each side of the pond plus feeding the pigs and
the dogs and cats and chickens and horses and hauling
buckets of coal into the house and setting them next to
our old coal furnace Then we grabbed brooms and
swept snow off the pond Got a tobacco stick each and
several puck size lumps of coal out of the coal shed
Then as snow drifted and the wind howled for hours
we played
tobacco sticks coal pucks ice hockey on our frozen pond

Square Bales Ain't Square and Neither Am I

Any old farm girl or boy will tell you
square bales ain't square and neither am I
Square bales are rectangular
and wrapped with grass strings
A fractal I am I love to play with the math of poetry
I live in and beyond dimensions 1 and 2 and 3
Oh the geometry of clouds and coastlines
2.78 and 3.14 and 4.73
When I was a boy I made up poems and songs
I sang them as I walked across the fields
The 723rd bale of 125 pound wet bean hay weighs a ton
Mama drove our 1010 John Deere tractor
while my brother Brad and I took turns
on the trailer then on the ground
loading in the field unloading at the barn
There's an art a dance a song to lifting and loading
125 pound rectangular bales of wet bean hay
Use your legs and back and arms equally
Cows love it but farm girls and boys
agree that the hardest work on the farm
in summer is hauling wet bean hay
Growing up on a farm was a gift
I learned to work hard without complaining
I'm thankful for that now

If you happened to know me
when I was an old farm boy
you'll surely realize
square bales ain't square and neither am I
A fractal I am I love to play with the math of poetry
I live in and beyond dimensions 1 and 2 and 3
When I was a boy I made up poems and songs
I sang them as I walked across the fields
Now I'm a man and I still sing
Oh the geometry of clouds and coastlines
2.78 and 3.14 and 4.73

Mourning My Father

We were hard on each other
Years after his death
there are times
during the day
in the night
I am hard on him still
Yet despite my echoing anger
I have always loved him
And there are times
in the night
during the day
when I am certain
he always loved me

Spadge Tooley Had Webbed Fingers

Once upon a time
When I was a boy
Mama took my brother Brad and me
To check on Spadge and his brother Jack
When we got out of the car Mama yelled
"Spadge! Jack!"
We heard them yell
"We're down here!"
Sounded like they were deep in a cave
We made our way around back of the house
Mama yelled "Where are you?"
Spadge yelled "We're down here, in the cistern!"
It was a hot day
Spadge and Jack had lowered a wooden ladder
Down into the cistern to cool off
They climbed out
Spadge said "Well hello Greta! Howdy boys!
You all come on in!"
I thought he was inviting us
To climb down into the cistern
But he turned and headed to the house
In the living room Mama said
"How pretty!"
She picked up the little pink and purple
Porcelain vase

Spadge said "You wanna buy it?"
He added "Mama bought it from gypsies
come through here years back."
Spadge was always needing money
For cigarettes and beer
Mama paid him 2 dollars for it
She kept that vase for years
I wondered if Spadge's Dad was a duck
He had webbed fingers
We all liked Spadge and Jack
Spadge was a storyteller
He helped Granddaddy and Daddy out
Whenever they needed help
To listen to Spadge you'd think he was lazy
He said "I don't know what this country's coming to.
It's getting to where a man
can't earn a living without working."
But Spadge was a hard worker.
He helped Granddaddy move the big old house
All the way from Olaton to Centertown
Then he used an ax to hand shape the rafters
Spadge and Jack mostly provided for themselves
by hunting and fishing and clearing timber
Spadge and Jack would go to the bottoms
Cut the trees and burn them
Clearing land for farming
Neither one of them had middle knuckles
But they could use an ax or a saw
It never seemed to bother them

They could roll a cigarette real tight
Out of a sack of Bull Durham
One day Brad and I were with Daddy
When he picked Jack up
Jack always walked everywhere
Jack was tall and skinny
He had a big beard
He reminded me of Abraham Lincoln
Daddy said "Jack it's a hot day.
Would you like a cold beer?
But I don't have an opener."
Jack said "I just happen to have one."
Jack always wore an opener
At the end of a string
Around his neck
Jack said "You never know when the son of man cometh."

Aunt Sis Was a Saint

Once upon a time
When I was a boy
Aunt Sis always wore a flower in her hair
I was 8 almost 9 when Granddaddy died
Granddaddy Raymond Render was her brother
Aunt Sis had Granddaddy's body
In her living room
In a coffin
People came from miles around
To visit and bring cakes and pies and food
Aunt Sis was married to Byron Igleheart
Byron was a hard working farmer
He was a good man
Aunt Sis and Byron lived on a farm outside Matanzas
They took Granddaddy to Walton's Creek Baptist Church
For the funeral
A thousand people lined the road
The church was packed
We buried Granddaddy in the Walton's Creek Graveyard
Mamaw is buried next to him now
After Byron died Aunt Sis moved to Centertown
That's when I started visiting her more often
Sometimes when she was talking
Her eyes rolled back in her head
Her eyelids closed

And the tone of her voice changed
She sounded different
Like she was somewhere far away
Talking about life and spiritual matters
Sometimes quoting the Bible
At the Centertown Baptist Church
Aunt Sis sat 3rd pew on the far right side
From time to time she'd stand up
Right in the middle of Brother Holladay's sermon
And her eyes would roll back then close
And she'd start talking like she did
When I sat with her at her home
And what she said was directly related
To what Brother Holladay had been preaching about
But she always took the subject deeper
To some holy and sacred place
That Brother Holladay hadn't reached
Aunt Sis never ceased to astonish me
In some deep and mysterious way
When ragamuffin vagabond dirty filthy hungry kids
Walked by her house
She opened her front door
I never knew how she knew they were out on the street
She invited them in
And gave them a bath then cut their hair
Then fed them then gave them a Bible
And sent them on their way
With her blessings
Aunt Sis was a saint

Otley Casteel

Once upon a time
When I was a young man
Daddy said "I want to tell you something
I've never told anyone but your Mother.
I was born during The Great Depression.
Times were hard.
But the man I'm telling you about
Was a portly gentleman
Who lived on Rough River.
His humble dwelling consisted of two rooms
On a hill overlooking the river.
He was married to a silent woman
Who worshipped him.
They had no children.
His wife was never seen
Unless he called her
Or gave her an order
Which she obeyed without question.
Day and night he roamed the hills.
If anything was stolen he got the blame.
But he paid no mind.
He strutted around like a millionaire.
He had a deep impressive voice.
He was always optimistic.
Had he lived another time

He might have been a success.
To hear him tell it
His fox hounds were always the best.
His horse was the fastest
And the best at pulling a heavy load.
There was always a boat tied
On his side of the river.
But he was smart.
If he was accused of stealing
A boat that showed up
Tied to his dock
He would say
He had caught it drifting downstream.
And maybe he had.
One day he found a nest of wild duck eggs
On the river bank.
He put them in his hat
And took them home.
His wife was sick in bed.
He told her since she was going
To have to stay in bed for a while
He would put the eggs in bed with her
And she could hatch them.
She didn't say a word.
His wife would shine his cracked and worn shoes
And iron his shirt so he looked his best.
He had straight hair slicked down tight
And he bounced when he walked.
He loved to shoot pool.

He would saddle his sorrel mare
And ride to town Saturdays
And stay until midnight.
Sometimes the boys
Turned his horse loose.
She would go on home
And he would have to walk.
If things got rough enough
He ran moonshine whiskey.
But the thing I remember most
About him happened years later.
The phone rang late one cold winter night.
I picked it up and it was Otley.
He said he remembered
When I was a boy
And he wanted someone to talk to.
He said he had been sick
And had already died
And gone to a place
He thought I might call Heaven
But had permission to return
And talk to someone about his life
And what it was like since he had passed over.
For two hours we talked about the other side
About the angels
And about some people we knew
That he had met again.
The next morning before work
I drove to town

And asked if anyone
Had heard from Otley.
His body had been found
The day before by Spadge Tooley.
Otley apparently had been dead for three days.
He died alone in his little two room home
Overlooking Rough River."
And that was the end of the story.
I asked Daddy
"Why did Otley call you and not someone else?"
Daddy turned and walked to the barn.
He never said another word
About Otley Casteel.

Learning to Swim
in the Deepest River in the World

I learned how to swim when I was 13
Daddy threw me into the Green River
The Green River
is the deepest river in the world
Daddy, Brad, and I went camping
and fishing with some of Daddy's friends
I knew it wasn't gonna be the best trip
when I realized I'd pitched my pup tent
over a patch of stinkweed
We caught a prehistoric gar fish
which I thought surely must be
a freshwater swordfish
We stayed up late
sitting round the campfire
Me listening to the men tell fishing tales
and other stories about the old days
and the strange people
who lived in those ancient and unsafe times
The next morning
we caught and cooked fish
over the campfire then
Daddy looked at me and said
"Ronnie, it's time you learn how to swim boy."
I just about choked on the big mouth bass

I was enjoying for breakfast
Cause you see
Well ever since I was a 5 year old boy
I'd heard stories of the giant catfish
that live in abandoned school buses
at the bottom of the Green River
the deepest river in the world
and I'd seen swarms of
killer poison water moccasins
churning pooling swarming
in coves of the Green River
and I'd read about the woman
who was skiing
and let go of the rope
and ended up dying
in a nest of water moccasins
and I'd heard the stories
about folks who got caught
in the underwater currents
and were never seen or heard from again
So when Daddy threw me from the rocky banks
into the deepest river in the world
I went down a ways
until my ears started popping
I reckon about 10 feet
but not too far before
I started working my arms and legs hard
to get my ass back to the top
then to the bank

and crawl out of the Green River
Growing up on a Kentucky farm
I spent a lot of enjoyable time
in and on ponds and creeks
and the Rough and Green Rivers
but none of those memories
stick out sharp in my mind
like the morning I learned how to swim
in the deepest river in the world

Kentucky Blues

"I am a poor wayfaring stranger
A wand'rin' thru this vale of woe
But there's no sickness, toil, or danger,
In that bright land to which I go.
I'm going there to see my mother,
I'm going there no more to roam;
I'm going over Jordan
I'm only going over home"

From Kentucky he came to east Chicago railyard to work
he was   gone
And at night   after   fourteen hour days
    Gideon's Bible and The Cheapest Wine   warmed
       body and soul   sacred ceremony
in ramshackle bedbug newspaper walled beer sign neon hotel
Within eyeshot of "the yard"
    Not far to lumber on frigid morn

Early evening
    thru the night
       all night
the wind whispers cries wails sings
    to her
       And thru the cracks
          of her attic walls

   she listens she listens she listens
 And when the wind don't blow
   she turns an ear
     to the voice coming to her
        thru the stillness
 thru the stillness of gnarled cedar and pine
   Blanketing like shrouds the old
     gray weathered wood slatted farmhouse
       Nestled deep in this coal barren wilderness

And she turns an ear
       to the voice coming to her
         thru the stillness
           of cedar and pine
  And thru the stillness
    she turns and looks at his
gray rail man's hat hanging limp from 8 penny nail on wormwood wall
    His hat and railroad manual were all
      he brought home the last time
  But that first Christmas visit
        from east Chicago and his new job
he brought her a blue calico dress and red sweater with pearl buttons
    Carried on the train with gifts for all
      He and they all proud
        of him a man no longer boy

But always hard worker of farm and mine
    in this pioneer Kentucky land
But now he returns again   so soon   unexpected
         Returns   eternal
    presence   Home   for good   His body
  From east Chicago railyards he comes
    His body crushed between coal cars   coal
And like the bituminous gold shipped from Kentucky to foreign parts
         he's delivered by train
  Long   wailing   whistle   signals   his   arrival
    Last stop of the L & N

And a year later   frail   tired   torn
               she drifts
                     Thru tears
        by candlelight she sees

She sees his spirit at top of attic stairs
      At foot of her bed   Calming real
    presence he moves closer Reaching to her
    his hand touches her forehead Her eyes close finally
            to deep dream sleep

The Loneliest Picture I've Ever Seen

Fatherhood duties done, standing, one last time,
before departing, into spirit, I see you, in the distance,
standing alone, at the top of the hill overlooking the farm,
woods behind, providing shade and comfort,
but all you see is the farm, pond churning with
blue and gray catfish, meadows grazed by red and white
Herefords, cows and bull, chickens and roosters clucking
and crowing round and in the coup, tall tasseled corn,
gleaming green soybeans, Mama and us kids,
Brad Paddy Edie Robin Velvet me, hoeing in the garden,
bird dogs in their pens, the old red barn, silver tin roof,
filled with hay and corn and the 1010 John Deere tractor,
and with broke down lawnmowers, harness, saddles,
tools tools tools, wasps, yellow jackets, mud daubers,
black snakes, kittens, puppies, spiders, cow manure,
coal black black coal in the shed, and in the barnyard
pigs, goats, horses, beehives, Kentucky wildflowers,
and trees, near and far, trees, maple, elm, oak, cedar,
pine, dogwood, redbud, sassafras, giant white barked
sycamore, and, resting in the midst of all this beauty,
our farmhouse, our farmhouse,
over the ever flowing seasons, spring summer fall winter,
our farmhouse grew, one room at a time, for years
an outhouse, then indoor plumbing, a back porch became
a kitchen, an unfinished attic birthed a small unfinished

bedroom, wind whistling singing through holes in walls,
conjuring the spirits of our dead relatives, loving kinfolk,
whispering, appearing to us, Brad and me, sleeping there,
in the attic, each night, our farmhouse, our home,
and home to relatives friends strangers, whoever knocked
was welcome, you and Mama made it so,
our coal and wood furnaced farmhouse,
always welcoming all, filled to overflowing with amazing
brilliant hued stories of birth, the journey, and death, pain
and beauty, tears, heartache, laughter and angelic music
singing Amazing Grace How Great Thou Art
morning noon night season into season embracing
letting go you hold now, pausing, before letting go,
finally moving on, your work done, mission accomplished,
you wait one final moment, you hold,
nestle all of it, all of us close to your heart, filled
overflowing with gratitude with thanks with
joyous tears, you hold us deep in your heart,
your soul as you, in the distance, stand now,
departing, alone, Fatherhood
duties done, standing, one last time before departing
into spirit, I see you, there you are, the strongest best man
I've ever known, there, clearly, I see you, in the distance,
my dear Father, my dear dear Father, and it's
the loneliest picture I've ever seen

Mama, a Poet's Heart in a Kentucky Girl

When I was a boy time and again
Always in a hurry I ran in through the back screen door

Of our old farmhouse looking for a ball or glove
And out of the corner of my eye I saw

Mama writing in her spiral notebook
Mama's work was never done

She worked night and day
But she always found time to write a few words

Then she'd hide her notebook away
To the kitchen the garden the yard the barn the field

To work she forever went
When I woke up in the mornings

When I went to bed at night
Mama was working working working

But I never once in all my life
Heard Mama complain

Late one night a few years ago
Reading Mama's handwritten notes I found

One written on the back of a torn envelope
The note was written to Daddy

It said "When all the children leave home
I'm going to become a writer"

Things have changed so much for women
In the 87 years Mama has shared with us

But women still aren't fully equal to men
They're still paid less for doing the same jobs

And in some countries they're still slaves
But it sure made me happy that Mama

Was so excited to write a book with me
Mama's always been a writer

And in 2015
Greta Render Whitehead became

A published author with a book in her name
Mama: a poet's heart in a Kentucky girl

Arriving

Not many deer crossed the road back then
but life was wild I remember the call
October 1959 I was nearly 9 Mama was
in the house on the phone I could hear her
crying moaning talking I was standing behind
the barn It was hotter than hot I started praying
for Granddaddy to live To be all right I was just
a boy But Granddaddy was special to me Real
special He was wild like the deer that appeared
and vanished when Granddaddy drove 90 miles
per hour on Highway 261 between Fordsville
and Hardinsburg Heading from Centertown to
Valley Station Going home Me riding shotgun
Windows down Flying on old Kentucky country
backroads So many times Granddaddy stopped
at the little McQuady grocery near Rough River to get me
soda crackers and ginger ale cause back then
I got car sick but Granddaddy only laughed and
smiling talked to me like I was real and not just
a kid I remember a 6 pack of beer on the floor
in the back and a pint of whiskey in the glove box
Granddaddy was real When he breathed
the earth breathed He moved things He was
a grader operator building the Watterson
Expressway around Louisville He was a barber

He cut hair He made records He traveled and
sang on radio stations and at concerts He
yodeled He cleared the land the rundown
farm he bought that had belonged to his
Mom and Dad my Great Grandparents Render
He went fox and coon hunting with his friends
in the middle of the night Always drinking
whiskey and telling stories that made the men
laugh I know cause I went with him whenever
I was allowed Granddaddy didn't preach but
his life was a sermon He was spirit Holy Spirit
No matter what anyone says So I drive fast
with the windows down and I don't wear a seat belt
and I'm taking a hard curve with the long wind
and the tall green trees and the turquoise sky
and the energy comes to me and it fills me and
I feel what Granddaddy felt The energy of life of sex
of love of family of longing and I smile and I cry
on this hot August morn and I know that somehow
Granddaddy's spirit is still here with me and my
head and my body want to explode but I hold
on to the wheel with all my might moving from
day into night and back to light finally finally
arriving

Kentucky Haiku

1

In Kentucky
always
I go too far

2

In Kentucky
I pass fast
on one lane bridges

3

In Kentucky
my skin turns
blue & I holler

4

In Kentucky
smoke the grass
sip the woman

5

In Kentucky
I take deadly
risks daily

6

In Kentucky
I won't live
much longer

7

In Kentucky
I feel like
I'm finally dyin'

8

In Kentucky
my Mom
was a prisoner

9

In Kentucky
my Dad
hoed tobacco

10

In Kentucky
I climb to top
of maple tree

11

In Kentucky
I wait for relatives
from Louisville

12

In Kentucky
I don't go
to the Derby

13

In Kentucky
springtime lie down
in orange sagebrush

14

In Kentucky
with old Blue
watch white clouds

15

In Kentucky
I married
the real Pippi

16

In Kentucky
my heart
was healed

17

In Kentucky
moon shines
comets are loud

18

In Kentucky
music
is mountainous

19

In Kentucky
my body burns
on funeral pyre

20

In Kentucky
my life travels
round the world

21

In Kentucky
I am
no more

About the Author

*Kentucky-born poet, writer, editor, publisher, scholar, activist **Ron Whitehead** is the author of 30 books and 40 cds.*

He has performed thousands of shows, with musicians and bands, round the world. He has produced over 3,000 poetry & music events, festivals, and non-stop 24 & 48 & 72 & 90 hour Insomniacathons throughout Europe and the USA.

He has published over 2,000 titles including works by Jack Kerouac, Allen Ginsberg, William S. Burroughs, Neal Cassady, Lawrence Ferlinghetti, Gregory Corso, Herbert Huncke, David Amram, Diane di Prima, Amiri Baraka, Ed Sanders, Anne Waldman, Hunter S. Thompson, Andy Warhol, Yoko Ono, Jim Carroll, Bono, Robert Hunter, Lee Ranaldo, Frank Messina, Birgitta Jonsdottir, Douglas Brinkley, E. Ethelbert Miller, Michael Dean Odin Pollock, Jan Kerouac, John Updike, Rita Dove, Eithne Strong, Theo Dorgan, President Jimmy Carter, Seamus Heaney, Thomas Merton, Robert Lax, Edvard Munch, Knut Hamsun, Jean Genet, James Laughlin, Brother Patrick Hart, Wendell Berry, His Holiness The Dalai Lama and many others. He wrote the poem Never Give Up with The Dalai Lama.

When not traveling the world he home bases at his hermitage on Cherokee Road in The Highlands of Louisville, Kentucky. You can contact the author through his website: www.tappingmyownphone.com or by email: ronwhiteheadpoet@gmail.com.

Made in the USA
Middletown, DE
15 April 2022